DuetTime® Piano

Christmas

Level 2
One Piano, 4 Hands

This book belongs to: _____

Arranged by

Nancy and Randall Faber

Production: Frank and Gail Hackinson
Production Coordinator: Marilyn Cole
Design: Gwen Terpstra Design, San Francisco
Music Editor: Edwin McLean
Engraving: Tempo Music Press, Inc.

FABER
PIANO ADVENTURES®
3042 Creek Drive
Ann Arbor, Michigan 48108

A NOTE TO TEACHERS

Christmas is a time for sharing with others. **DuetTime® Piano Christmas** provides your students the opportunity of sharing beautiful Christmas songs—as partners at the keyboard!

The Level 2 duet book uses the keys of C major, G major, and D minor. Although students often play in a 5-finger position, circled finger numbers indicate any change of hand position. Pedaling marks are indicated throughout the secondo part.

The arrangements frequently move the melody from one player to another. This sharing of the melody between players offers each pianist a chance to be both soloist and accompanist, providing a special opportunity to work on dynamics and ensemble.

DuetTime® Piano Christmas, Level 2 is part of the *DuetTime® Piano* series arranged by Faber and Faber for one piano (4 hands), from primer through intermediate levels.

Following are the levels of the supplementary library which lead from *PreTime®* to *BigTime®*.

PreTime® Piano	(Primer Level)
PlayTime® Piano	(Level 1)
ShowTime® Piano	(Level 2A)
ChordTime® Piano	(Level 2B)
FunTime® Piano	(Level 3A–3B)
BigTime® Piano	(Level 4)

Each level offers books in a variety of styles, making it possible for the teacher to offer stimulating material for every student. For a complimentary detailed listing, e-mail faber@pianoadventures.com or write us at the mailing address below.

Visit **www.PianoAdventures.com**.

Helpful Hints:

1. Students should be encouraged to set a steady pulse for one or two measures before beginning.

2. Help the student recognize whether he or she is playing the melody or harmony; then the piano team can strive for correct balance. (Melodies are indicated by the placement of lyrics, which are not intended to be sung.)

3. A student recording of one or more of the selections on cassette tape can make a wonderful holiday gift for parents or friends. Such a recording can show achievement, and serve as a musical keepsake.

ISBN 978-1-61677-038-9

TABLE OF CONTENTS

Jingle Bells 4

We Wish You a Merry Christmas 8

We Three Kings of Orient Are 10

Fum, Fum, Fum 14

French Carol *(Il est né)* 16

O Christmas Tree *(O Tannenbaum)* 20

Angels We Have Heard on High 22

There's Something Under the Christmas Tree 26

Music Dictionary 28

Jingle Bells

Secondo

Words and Music by
J. Pierpont

With excitement

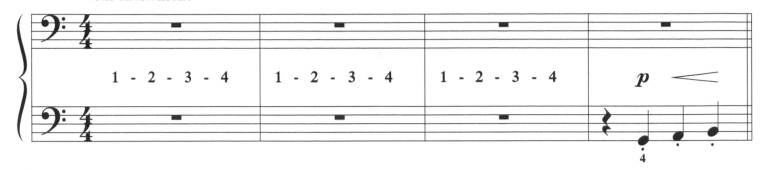

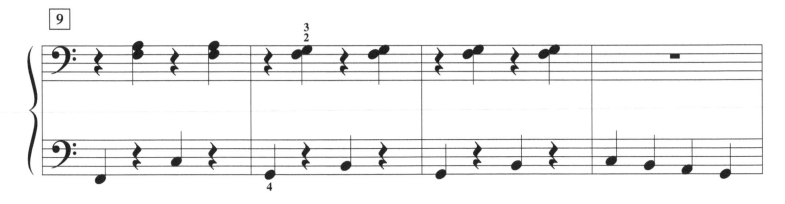

Jingle Bells

Primo

Words and Music by
J. Pierpont

With excitement

8va

f

5 *loco*

mf Dash - ing through the snow in a one - horse o - pen sleigh;

9

O'er the fields we go, laugh - ing all the way.

13

Turn page with R.H.

Bells on bob - tail ring, mak - ing spir - its bright; What

FF1038

Secondo

We Wish You a Merry Christmas

Secondo

Traditional English Carol

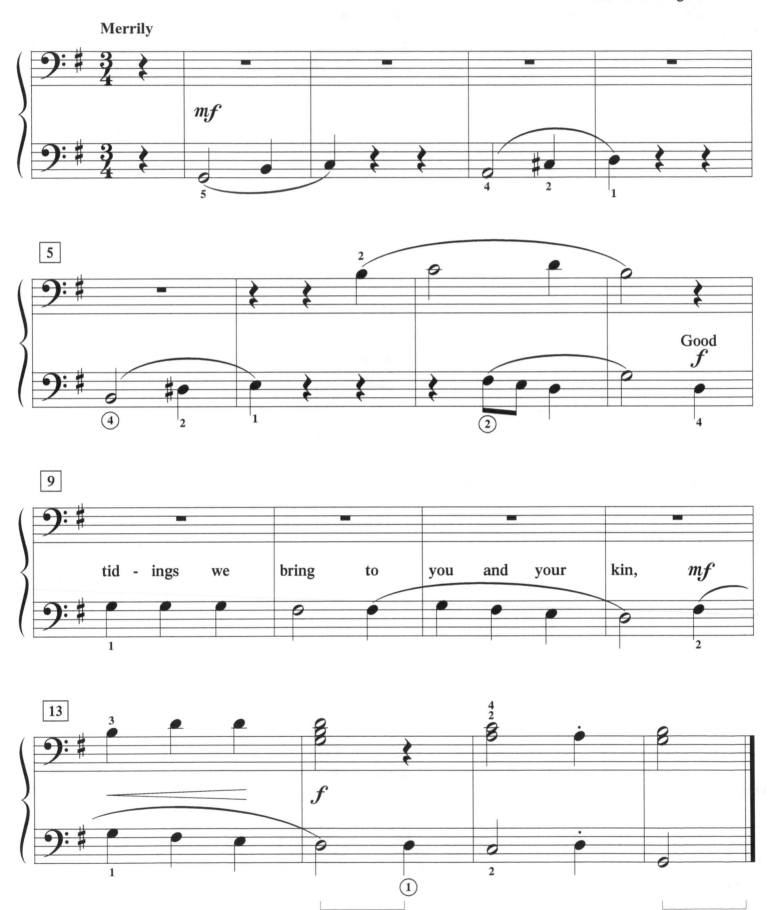

We Wish You a Merry Christmas

Primo

Traditional English Carol

We Three Kings of Orient Are

Secondo

Words and Music by
J. H. Hopkins, Jr.

We Three Kings of Orient Are

Primo

Words and Music by
J. H. Hopkins, Jr.

FF1038

Secondo

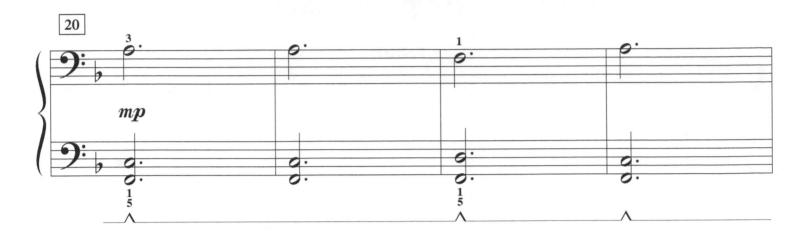

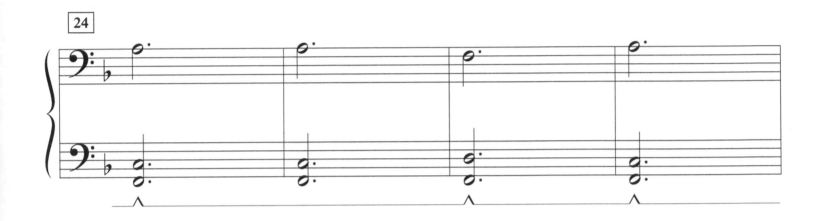

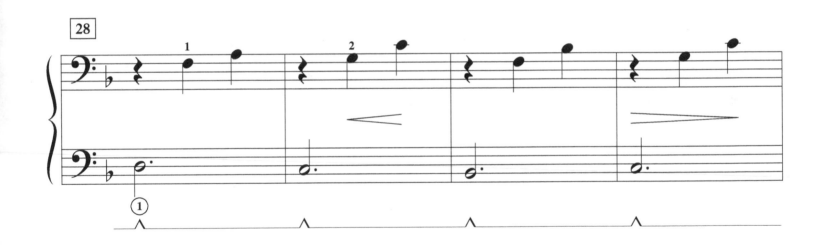

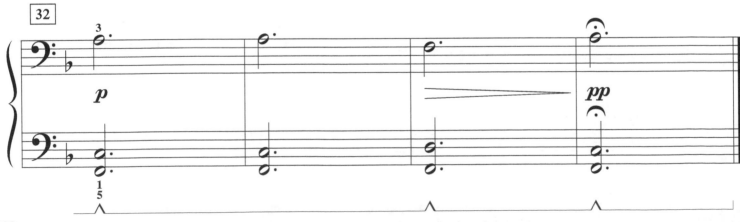

Primo

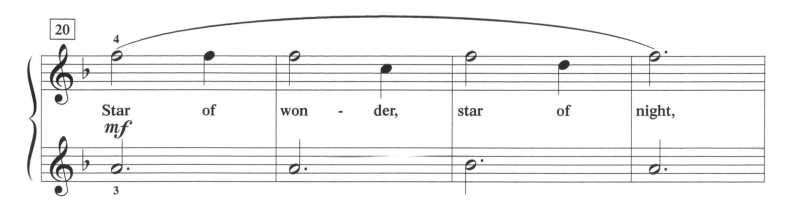

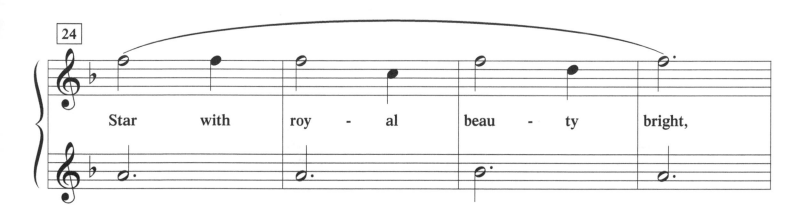

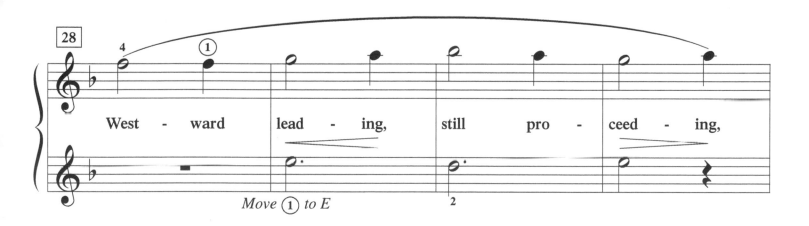

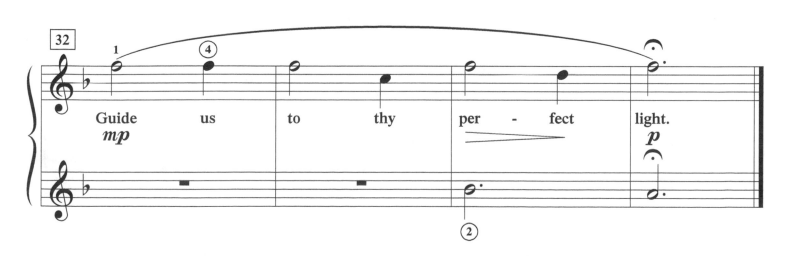

14

Fum, Fum, Fum

Secondo

Spanish Carol

Fum, Fum, Fum

Primo

Spanish Carol

FF1038

French Carol
(Il est né)
Secondo

Traditional French Carol

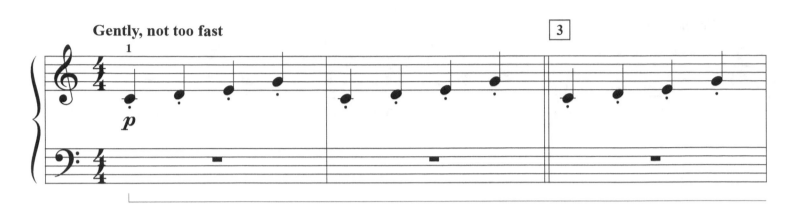

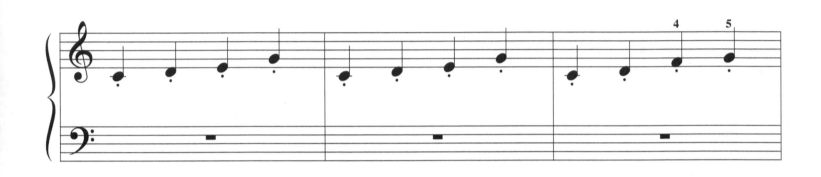

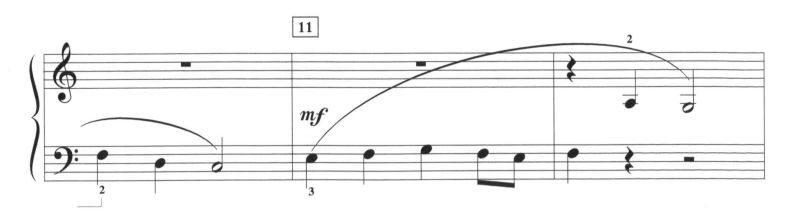

FF1038

French Carol
(Il est né)
Primo

Traditional French Carol

(Turn page with L.H.)

FF1038

Secondo

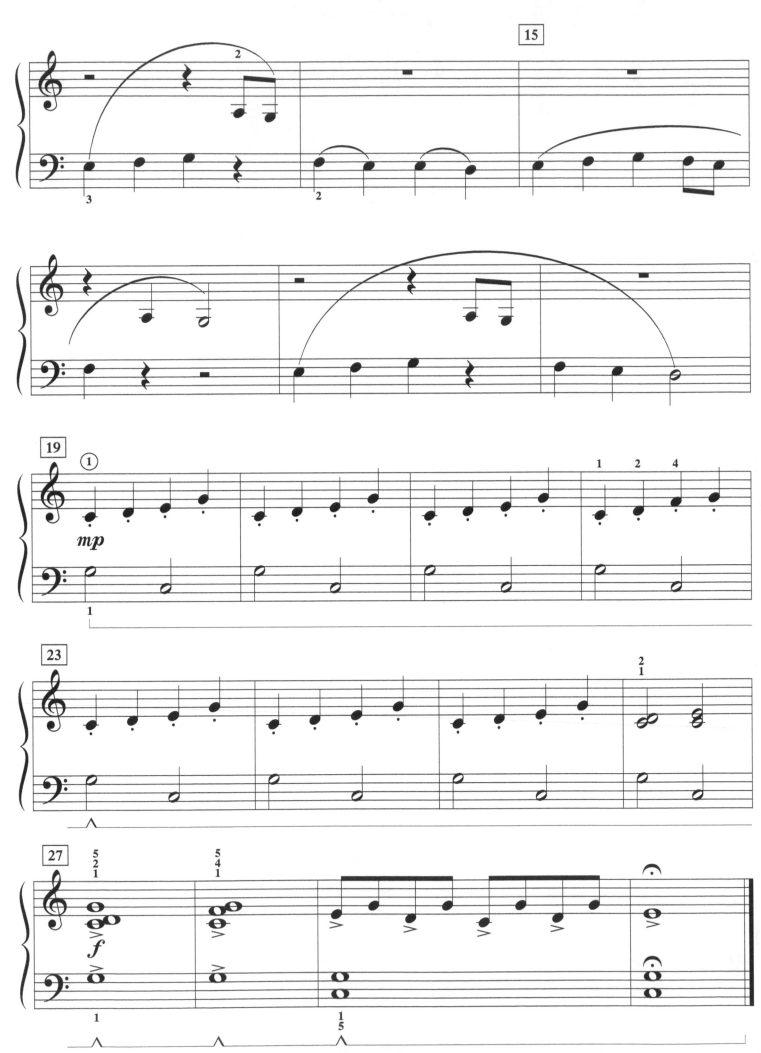

O Christmas Tree
(O Tannenbaum)
Secondo

Traditional German Carol

O Christmas Tree
(O Tannenbaum)
Primo

Traditional German Carol

With majesty

Both hands 8ᵛᵃ higher throughout

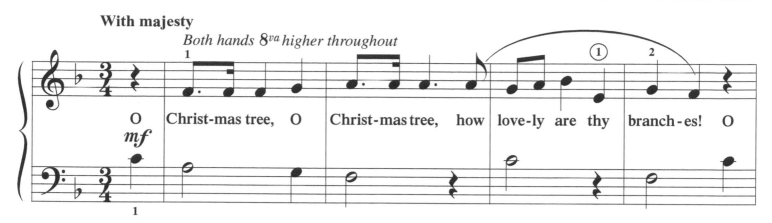

O Christ-mas tree, O Christ-mas tree, how love-ly are thy branch-es! O

Christ-mas tree, O Christ-mas tree, how love-ly are thy branch - es!

Christ-mas tree, O Christ-mas tree, how love-ly are thy branch-es!

FF1038

Angels We Have Heard on High

Secondo

Traditional

Angels We Have Heard on High

Primo

Traditional

Secondo

(ped. optional)

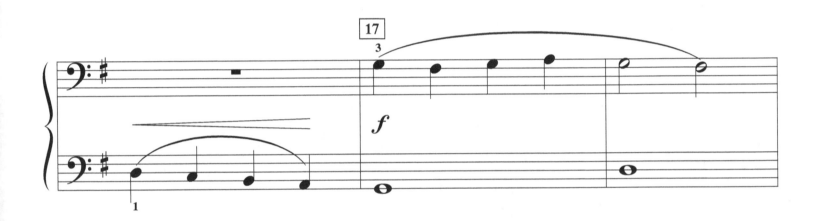

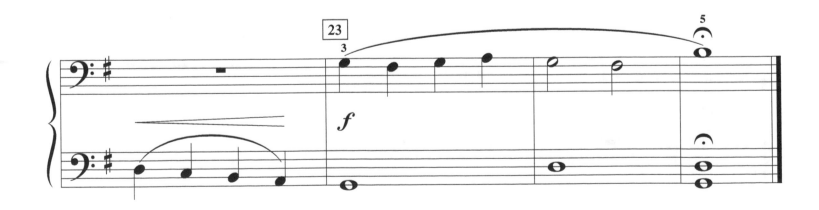

Glo - - - - - - - - - -

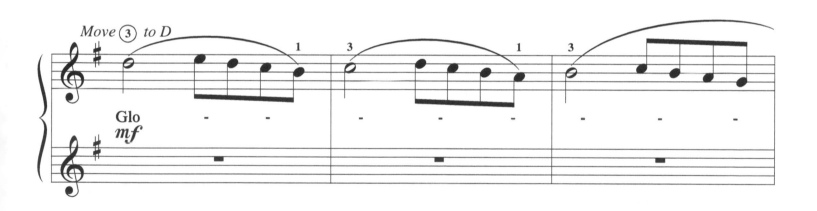

- ri - a in ex - cel - sis De - o,

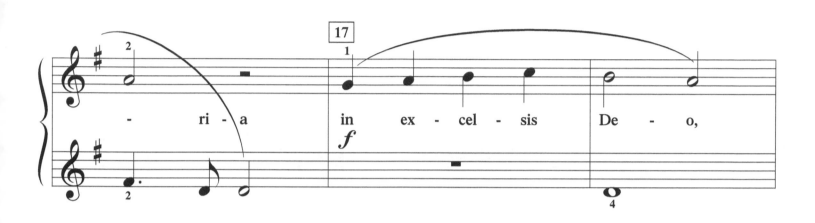

Move ③ to D

Glo - - - - - - - - - -

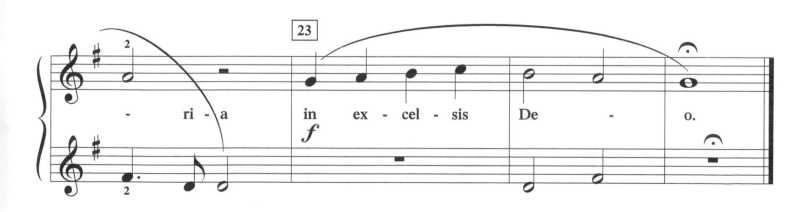

- ri - a in ex - cel - sis De - o.

There's Something Under the Christmas Tree

Secondo

Lyrics by
Jennifer MacLean

Music by
Nancy Faber and Randall Faber

With a playful swing

Might have green hair!

Ho, ho, ho!

There's Something Under the Christmas Tree

Primo

Lyrics by
Jennifer MacLean

Music by
Nancy Faber and Randall Faber

With a playful swing

FF1038

MUSIC DICTIONARY

pp	*p*	*mp*	*mf*	*f*	*ff*
pianissimo	*piano*	*mezzo piano*	*mezzo forte*	*forte*	*fortissimo*
very soft	soft	medium soft	medium loud	loud	very loud

crescendo (cresc.)
get louder

diminuendo (dim.)
get softer

Primo		The first part in duet playing.
Secondo		The second part in duet playing.

SIGN	TERM	DEFINITION
>	**accent**	Play this note louder.
	a tempo	Return to the original *tempo* (speed).
⌢	*fermata*	Hold this note longer than usual.
	loco	"Place." Play as written. (A reminder to end 8*va*.)
8*va* – ¬	ottava	Play one octave higher than written. When 8*va* – ⌐ is below the staff, play one octave lower.
⌊___⌋	**pedal marking**	Depress the damper pedal (right foot pedal) after you play the note or chord; release at the end of the pedal mark.
___∧___	**pedal change**	Lift the pedal on the beat and depress immediately after.
rit.	*ritard*	Gradually slow down. Short for *ritardando*.
	sempre	Always.
⌒	**slur**	Shows a musical phrase. Connect these notes.
•	*staccato*	Play notes marked *staccato* detached, disconnected.

Level 2B Supplementary Material by Faber & Faber

Piano Adventures® Popular Repertoire	FF1259
Piano Adventures® Christmas (with "sightreading stocking stuffers")	FF1140
Piano Adventures® Gold Star Performance (with online audio)	FF1605
Preparatory Piano Literature (Developing Artist Library - with online audio)	FF1027
Piano Literature Book 1 (Developing Artist Library - with online audio)	FF1030

ChordTime® Piano Series:

Popular	FF1004
Classics	FF1020
Favorites	FF1014
Rock 'n Roll	FF1021
Jazz & Blues	FF1046
Ragtime & Marches	FF1133
Hymns	FF1003
Children's Songs	FF1041
Christmas	FF1005
Jewish Favorites	FF1192

Once Upon a Rainbow, Book 2 (colorful solos by Nancy Faber)	FF1104
Discover Beginning Improvisation	FF1051
Discover Blues Improvisation (with online audio)	FF1155CD
I Can Read Music, Book 2 (a notespeller)	FF1060
PracticeTime Assignment Notebook	FF1167

Achievement Skill Sheets:

No. 1 Major 5-finger Patterns and Cross-Hand Arpeggios	AS5001
No. 2 Minor 5-finger Patterns and Cross-Hand Arpeggios	AS5002
No. 3 One-Octave Major Scales and Arpeggios	AS5003
No. 7 Elementary I-V-I Cadences	AS5007

Achievement Solo Sheets:

Cat Prowl	A2027
Classic Sonatina	A2005
Jazz Pizzazz	A2030
Land of Dreams	A2031
The Notorious Pirate	A2023
The Little Tin Soldier (Duet)	AD3004

ABOUT THE FABERS

Nancy and Randall Faber have combined their backgrounds as composer and performer to become leading supporters of piano teachers and students. The husband and wife team has authored over 300 publications, including the bestselling *Piano Adventures®* method and the *PreTime® to BigTime® Piano Supplementary Library*. Their innovative, student-centered approach continues to enjoy an unprecedented response from teachers and students worldwide.

Nancy Faber was named "Distinguished Composer of the Year" by the Music Teachers National Association for her award-winning composition *Tennessee Suite for Piano and String Quartet*. Her flute quartet *Voices from Between Worlds* was the winning composition for the National Flute Association's Professional Chamber Music Competition. She was commissioned by the Music Teachers National Association for its Year of Collaborative Music. Nancy's music has been heard on network television, public radio, and in piano recitals of teachers around the world. She studied composition with Joan Tower, William Albright, Charles Ruggiero, and British composer Nicholas Maw. Piano studies were at the Eastman School and Michigan State University, where she was honored with the Distinguished Alumni Award in 2015.

Randall Faber has performed extensively as a classical pianist and lectures on musical artistry and talent development around the world. His performances have aired on television and public radio. He was a master teacher for the World Piano Pedagogy Conference, the Music Teachers National Association Conference, and the National Conference on Keyboard Pedagogy, and has presented as guest artist at universities throughout North America and Asia. Randall holds three degrees from the University of Michigan and a Ph.D. in education and human development from Vanderbilt University.

The Fabers advocate piano study not only for personal expression and performance success, but also as a vehicle for the student's creative, cognitive, and personal development. Their philosophy is reflected in their writing, their public appearances, and in their own teaching.